CONSENSUAL GENOCIDE

Leah Lakshmi Piepzna-Samarasinha

We acknowledge the support of the Canada Council for our
publishing program.
We also acknowledge support from the Ontario Arts Council.

 Canada Council   Conseil des Arts
for the Arts   du Canada

 ONTARIO ARTS COUNCIL
CONSEIL DES ARTS DE L'ONTARIO

Cover art by Chamindika Wanduragala

Author photograph by Richelle Forsey

Library and Archives Canada Cataloguing in Publication

Piepzna-Samarasinha, Leah Lakshmi, 1975-
    Consensual genocide : poems / Leah Lakshmi Piepzna-Samarasinha.

ISBN 1-894770-29-3

    1. Minority lesbians--Poetry. I. Title.

PS8631.I46C65 2006   C811'.6   C2006-901481-7

Printed in Canada by Coach House Printing

TSAR Publications
P.O. Box 6996, Station A
Toronto, Onatrio M5W 1X7
Canada

www.tsarbooks.com

this is for my family
lost and stolen
blood and chosen

Contents

eating a $5 plate of string hoppers, I think of my father

snoozing in front of Seinfeld on the beige on beige recliner
his belly folds   after years
of american chop suey, hamburgers and Michelob
Nothing
he really wanted to eat
was ever on the shelves
of Iandolli's or the Big D
I think of that man
who cried three times in my life
once when *appamma* died
once when our dog died
and once when I sent him
a 99-cent package of tamarind candy
and he called me long distance after Ma went to bed
weeping   from tasting tamarind
for the first time in thirty years

a love poem for Sakia Gunn

Sakia   looking at your face on the memorial website
I know I could've fallen in love with you
so easy when I was sixteen
You could've met my eyes just once
wearing rainbow rings that were brave, not cheesy
We could've been taking that late train back to Newark
 falling sticky stars all over each other in the vinyl seat
my titties poking out   pussy humming
stupid fearless

When I was 16 I gave blow jobs behind the high school
I would do anything   to feel my breasts buzzing
When I was 18 I rode the N train home at 5 AM
smelling like Night Queen in a bra under a bomber jacket
I acted crazy   I stared at the ad in front of me
I yelled my head off
Living was risky anyway
so I did what I needed to do
I was horny for the revolution
but I didn't have it

Did your girlfriend have your head in her lap that day?
Were you dancing to somebody's boombox
throwing shade and fixing nail tips
as the water kissed and slapped the piers
as the cops erected fences around bodies
but did not stop the men who asked you home?

Sakia
you were just trying to get home
We
are all trying to get there
with you
to that place   where we can suck our breath
all the way down
where they do not end us

in memory and respect, for Sakia Gunn
Black queer youth, born 1987, murdered May 11, 2003

2

Persistence

I never knew anything
I asked my father again and again
"What are we?"
His face was a slammed door
"Why do you want to know?"
his only answer

My mother confused me with names
Ceylon   Malaya   Singapore
"Your father is mostly Dutch," my mother said
"and so are you"
Later came
"Daddy's brown   Mommy's white
you're beige"
"If they ask, say you're beige."

I faked a lot of things growing up
I got straight As doing my homework on the bus
I was the daughter of a woman who raised bullshit to a high art
on the phone to the electric company   to the neighbors
to herself and me

When I was 18 and walking Brooklyn streets
I could turn into anything that was safe for a minute
Arab   Latina   Jewish
Asia was a huge continent
barely on the map
Ceylon didn't exist
and did we come from that new country
Sri Lanka
that took its place?

There were no explanations
but my persistence
I dug the crumpled genealogies
out of the Massachusetts attic
dug the stories out of my parents
with coconut spoons   my hands

One day when I was 21
my father was filling out the census form
at the dining room table
I asked him   one last time
"Dad, what are we?"
He snapped, "Tamil!"
His voice broke
as he ran from the room

But that was all I needed:
One word
One name
A place to begin

landmine heart

there is an unexploded land mine heart in me
waiting for a footstep   a breath
for troop movements   a tsunami
a woman's walk
a storm that will make these waves rise
explode everything we have buried

there is an unexploded land mine heart in us
under every breast   chest
waiting for breath
tears   a moan
to crack the land open
and let the stories come walking
out of the scar

At the naturopath's

She says
You have a scar on the back of your vaginal wall
It looks very old
and very well healed

This is as close as I will get
to a videotape sent by God
with *What Happened*
written on the label

This has nothing to do
with courts and what will
stand up in them

I see
pink   folded   tiny
spark   rip
bathroom tiles
wrong   lightning
four year old body
mine

what I have always felt on the inside of my body
what I always saw on the inside of closed eyes

I feel that vein standing up inside me
I slide off the table   pull on my pants
leave with that gift:
someone else has seen
what no one ever did

lots of reasons why I loved you

the way you rode your bike to some fifty dollar foot fetish call
in your hoodie and leather jacket
headphones blasting the saddest Tupac songs
99 cent lipstick like a kid's crayon on your lips
the dusting of hair at your nape made my clit clench
coffee in one hand, cigarette in the other
the way you skidded short and blushed
when you saw me walking towards you
even though it made you late

the way when I said
"just cuz I was too freaked out to flirt on Friday" –
lotsa *fs* – "doesn't mean I don't want to fuck you"
 you looked up to the sky like *thank you*
before you grabbed me
the way you rode off with the memory of a handful of ass
my MAC Ultra Violet Lip Lacquer all over your face
to plop a cheap cherry wig on your head and fist some stupid john
without wiping your face

I couldn't make you laugh for
ninety days of fucking not
talking but when I did it was worth it
my clit caught in the gap in the front teeth
of your smile as you somersaulted off
the bed

dropping bombs

I want to be naked in your arms
to kiss you without shrapnel falling

but when I saw you
I knew loving you
would be too much a war
bombs exploding under our skins
from different continents
We can see exactly how each other
has been broken
but when we love
we want to remember
what has stayed whole.
I would be too naked in your arms
to kiss you without shrapnel falling

when I saw you you were bling and heart
the dream boy centerfold etched on my left ventricle.
I leaned over, showed cleavage, fluttered
I say we don't have to go too deep
it'll just be like a porn movie
but I fall in love after the first night
with anyone I am picky enuf
to choose

this time I don't say shit   am a good friend
don't cock my hip   bite my tongue
shop for groceries   listen to you talk about your wife's beauty

but I still wonder
if loving each other brown
will always tear our continents wide open
I dream a place
where I could touch you naked
and our kiss could turn back
every bomb that's ever fallen

white Australia

memory
is always what's gone
memory is always
the last thing that remains

My grandmother got us into Australia
when it was still "white Australia"
In 1965 anyone who wanted to get in
had to prove they were at least 98% white blood

My grandmother powdered her face
brought out the genealogies
from the Dutch Bugher Union
the Episcopalian Church of Colombo
She wasn't in them
but she smiled   hard
her eyes like a diamond drill
black   flinty   could cut you in half

When my grandmother aunties uncles and cousins left
they said they didn't miss Sri Lanka
that Sri Lanka wasn't what it used to be
They went to Melbourne
near the best lamprais and curry shop
settled in the best they could
with the 50 dollars they were allowed to take
times were hard   but at least it's still warm
she always said

in Melbourne
my grandmother aunties cousins uncles
realized they were brown
them   who had always been   faded
pale   and almost white

they realized it

9

when a lorry driver yelled as they walked down the street
they realized it
        as my grandmother's teaching certificate crumbled
to dust
they realized it   as the voices on the radio
railing against dirty immigrants grew louder
and louder

as flames engulfed *illankai*
our country was on fire   and they realized
they would grow old   die
in this country   far   from the one they said
was not like it used to be

As they grew up   my cousins got married
Some of them   married white
Some of them   married brown
and in the grandchildren's skins
changed before our eyes
  just the way   we had   five hundred years ago

memory   is always   what's gone
memory   is always
the last thing that stays

dreaming of the garden of eden

In the old days   back home
when a women got tired of her man
she'd make him take whatever he could carry
and send him packing   back to his mama's house
down the mountain

Now   women smile for the camera
as the state photographer snaps a picture
Lipton's tea garden
has cut down the mountain.
The Export Processing Zone throbs
like a heart
punched out of a country

I sit in Toronto and Brooklyn reading about these women
checking books out of the library til they were too overdue to return
I want all of this to be   in my silent father's memory
choked by the amber liquor that choked many of us;
arrack became Johnnie Walker in the countries we moved to.
maybe it's in his memory   the same way it's in mine
not the memories   of things I've lived
the ones carried   in my blood's thick water

We were the one Sri Lankan in Las Vegas, Worcester Mass,
Lancaster CA
like a bad joke no one's ever heard
We were one of the thousands after '83
surviving cargo holds and refugee camps
 Our aunties snapped at all of us
"*you* are Canadian! American! British! *You* could never..."

go back
to this island   shaped like a tear
There are reasons why everyone says no place
is as beautiful as home
This was where the Garden of Eden story came from

this green on green
was where paradise was

I don't know if when I go back
this place will seem like paradise or hell
or both:
my appamma's house filled with bullet holes
this earth dreaming memory
women who still smile
only when they want to
There is no paradise to go back to
just this place
rich and sharp as raw gems

tsunami song

It's the day after Christmas
I'm at my girlfriend's house
on her futon full up with
dirty socks   empty coffee cups   everything
(she's a lot messier than me but she has cable)
I am clicking channels   I am full
until I see them
my people
for the first time

I am used to no one being able to find my country on any map
We are like the Congo or Sudan
or any piece of land in North America
genocide that happens
and you say *Where? Pass the salt*

20 years of civil war never dented the headlines
but the day after Christmas
the surviving children of Batti and Colombo
of '83 and '56,
fill the malls
lined up outside
shoe and computer stores
security guards watching over consumer products
our relatives ruined their eyesight for
Then this wave hits my television
and I am transfixed
half a world away
and a block
from the dosa mahal

fifty years

This morning
words lie thrown dying
in a pool of blood in my choked throat
this morning the paper hands me the headline
prime minister empties the fishtank:
if she kills everyone
noone will be left to kill her

This morning   wet broken screaming
brown hips in mine
wake me up
wake me up to a genocide
I've never seen in the flesh
that won't leave my body alone.

and you
behind dishwashing machines, typewriters and taxi wheels
the lines around your eyes familiar as my own
what are we doing at this moment?
Sitting round the bigscreen on the busted couch
bottles and blunts smoking us out
from having to talk about it
Let's talk about anything else
but the houses burned   sisters begging
brothers buried in even mounds
This fire seals our mouths

This morning
chronic fatigue slips up on me
handing out flyers for seven bucks cash I'm grateful for
This morning keeping on going is sandpaper on my clit
This morning I don't wanna nod out on TV and fresh gear
Starbucks and Loblaws driving me to despair
Ain't gonna settle for survival in a stripped settled stolen land
this maximum security infotocracy
where they think they know everything

but I know Kali
shaking her hips and her guns
Her madness
her creation   her destruction
will rip us   our land   our hearts
in two

Operation Babylift

I've just been born. My mother is lying on her bed watching
Operation Babylift on TV. This is the story she will tell me for years
later on, watching the last effort of white Americans in world war
three part one, against the Vietnamese, taking their children. chil-
dren runafter helicopters, hang on to their bottom rungs as they lift
off. My mom is on morphine. Her cunt has been cut twice, vertically
like a normal episiotomy and sideways. They tell me this is to get
me out, to save my life. She's watching halfbreed kids get saved,
into america. White skin, Mickey Mouse, freeways, gasoline. She's
watching what she will do to me, clucking over those poor children.
Not belonging here or there. "So tragic, like the Ugandans, they
were stateless people – Idi Amin told them to leave, go back to
India. But they weren't Indian anymore, they were more British
than the British.

She's telling this to me later, the tape speeds up, it's 1987, I'm in the
passenger seat next to her in the Volvo, driving, she's telling me
that I'm not stateless, not brown except for a speck for flavor.
Garnish.

she asked me what my heart was like
and I said it was like sri lanka

If she asked me the state of my heart
I would say
that what I am capable of
is continuing
loving my way
through scar tissue

my country
where the head of the ruling party
said *since I came to power*
we have completely eliminated terror
The day after he won
20 Tamil youth were set on fire
There was a protest
The police shot two people.
some Sinhalese started burning houses and stores.
The MP who issued a mild statement was arrested at 1 AM

This has been going on for twenty years
but people still go on
feeding chickens
growing pumpkins
commuting to work

If she asked me the state of my heart
I would say
that what I am capable of
is continuing
I want to love my way through scar tissue

Welcome to Slave Island
(found poem)

Slave Island, Ceylon

"The high rise hotels and offices which have occupied the north-
ward jutting peninsula now leave no trace of what was known as
'Slave Island'.'Island' was a misnomer but slaves played a very real
part in the colonial history of Sri Lanka. In the Dutch period this
tongue of open veldt was known as Kaffir Veldt.

"The 'Kaffirs' – Africans from the east coast around Mozambique –
were brought to Sri Lanka for the first time by the Portuguese from
Goa in 1630. When the Dutch ousted the Portuguese they made use
of slave labor to build the fort in Colombo,
where there may have been 4,000 of them.

"Their numbers grew, but after an unsuccessful insurrection in the
18th century the Dutch decided to insist that all slave labor be
identifiably accommodated"

"The Kaffir Veldt was the nearest open space
on which special shanty houses could be built
and a nightly roll call was held to ensure that every slave was there
in 1807 Cordimer reports that the number of slaves had fallen to
7000
yet the British didn't abolish slavery til 1845.
nevertheless the name Slave Island has persisted"

good burgher girl

study hard in school
be white   or just one drop of tea in the milk   after all
doesn't your father sound like he went to Oxford?

all the time I was told
Dutch china and Ceylon tea
engineers clerks and teachers
rape smearing all our faces
above the smart frocks,
flirty looks, good marriages

stepgrandfather driving a rusted-out Rolls down the mountain
sucking gin and tonics from a gas can
steering with his knees

lying our way into white Australia
doing the limbo just under that line:
marrying dinkum Aussies and Tamil men
milk tea fading into milk
or into the strong tea we were bleached from

Auntie G's photo in the album
that's white in Sri Lanka? my friend said
she looks, you know...

I'm just like all those light brown girls with funny green eyes
in private schools and tea fields
all those girls walking down Melbourne streets hearing *Paki bitch*
in central Mass hearing *fuck me hot chica*
all the curly headed hazel eyed women   the world over

In the album see
my red rebel grandmother's face
your fist flower face in your 20s in the 30s

I'm just like you grandma
who brushed my face with her fingers once
before you turned away
to where your story ended
trapped in that marriage that saved you from
nothing but a bad reputation between your legs

I'm just like you only
I move
only this story won't end
with my good marriage to a boy with no
insanity in the family

I might be the generation
that flies home
to scatter my father's ashes
the man who never went back

I know I am another
seriously pretty woman
making everything happen
not suburban townhouse and husband
but my girl saying
you have the darkest eyes

mi vida loca, summer 1998

she kept saying
"I want your hair.
If you die, leave me your hair"
this Grenadian woman
owner of the hair salon
on the second floor
of a shit colored building
downtown drag strip
Toronto
summer 1998

I was handing out flyers for her
for $7 an hour cash
So what's a conscious half-masala girl
with Puerto Rican hair to do?
She told me she paid $2000 for her hair
already starting to drop   lose its loose curl
every time I came up to the water cooler they'd all be
sitting around, doing yellowjackets and she'd come over
shiny bright eyes 'n grab a fist full.

I couldn't afford sunblock that summer
was smearing myself with olive oil from the kitchen instead
I just kept getting browner and browner
and she'd look at me and be like
"You know what?
You look... mulatta!
Are you?"

Every day
white girls would come up the stairs for $2000 extensions.
On the street the crew from Two Spirit People of the First Nations
would flash by
one queen with waist length hair
would arch an eyebrow and say
honey, do your really think I need to do anything to this?
The cops were parked across the street
eating Somali falafels and glaring at me and

the guy handing out flyers for the souvlaki joint next door,
he kept telling me

he was born in Canada but grew up in NYC
kept asking if i knew about the Flying Dragons, he was big in the
Flying Dragons back home, he used to powder his nose for free all
the time, had a gatt and....
Kept asking me if he looked too feminine (he pointed to the huge
butterfly belt buckle on his crotch) he wasn't gay, everybody
thought he was gay, he kept going to this clubs to see these men
who dress as women, but that doesn't make him GAY, y'know,
but they wanted him to be in this male stripper contest, did I think
he should?

I just kept nodding and going "oh yeah, uh huh."
and going up for water
when I couldn't deal with saying
 "haircuts on special   discount hair styling"
one more time
after a while he'd get this smirk on his face
and ask me
"don't you feel like Rain Man?"

upstairs the staff'd be standing around
eyes red from excusing themselves to go to the john
and I'd ask to borrow two dollars so I could get a felafel
instead of walking home on nothing
and the boss would look annoyed and say
"why don't you just borrow ten?"

but when your salary is $660   your rent is $520
and your downstairs neighbor the conspiracy theorist
thinks the CIA planted some radiation in the backyard
and that's why all the organic vegetables   aren't growing
you can't play around
so I'd go back downstairs
buy a piece of pita for 35 cents
(plus tax)
get asked "are you black?
Sri Lanka, where's that?"

looking back
(or why I wasn't a famous poet at 19)

I see myself   stick thin girl
3 pounds of hair shellac head
rocking quietly   staring bug eyed
smiling please don't hit me   screaming FUCK YOU!
if I'm eating a 2 egg and homefry breakfast and a slice every day
 I must be ok
right?
right.
one glass of OJ has all the vitamins you need,
and I think I don't deserve any more
something
I never would've said
scampering through not a concrete
not a jungle
a steel forest
no trees that breathe green outside of cages
triple locked into a closet room
all I can feel is danger so I keep myself outside
nothing to hold onto on the inside
as I build myself a skeleton
one bone each month
I cling to the first rung of that ladder with one shaking hand
I don't have the muscle to push any higher
if I fall I'll never get another chance to come back up
I smile   wheedle   snarl
read anyone's mind in a second's time
find out what to turn into so they'll leave me alone
I don't find home here
just holes I can burrow into
tribes of broken children
brown skin reflected

These are the years I look like a junkie
but can't touch any drugs
I'm fucked up enough for free on my own

I riot in the streets, stay up all night, drink forties,
suck down more ash than's in the air
go months without speaking to any friend

there are daily phone calls home   it's like I never left
I throw a switch in my head to be the good daughter
who shouldn't be locked up
When are you coming home?
I don't want to is a whisper
The therapist says everyone has these weird
early childhood sexual memories
it doesn't mean anything
I dare to remember in the years of false memory
ask her if she knows who Audre Lorde is
A smile: *No. Why. Should I?*

I was too busy
learning my name
and how to walk without falling down the street
I was too focused on keeping on breathing
on not ending up in Bellevue
on not selling that hard bright sure
opal in my spine
that would lead me to become my own daughter
to
network
promote
rock tha mic
produce
charm
to even write down
the stories
I was transcribing from my bone

looking back #2 / snapshot in color

I float up Flatbush
a spangled hipped ghost
in my daisy dukes and lycra shimmer
Combat boots. One dandelion
behind my ear
Up to the cinema at 7th Ave and Flatbush
to see *Panther* with Retu.
My hips ache with turning back
the stares and grabs
My happiest moments spent
finding a stand of new trees in Prospect Park
curled hidden from sight
like I did when I was 7.
Everything you want to eat
costs money here
the land isn't free
and you have to buy something to piss or shit.
Clump clump. Boots hit the sidewalk
past the Palestinian grocery
where the blue-eyed woman smiles at me
past beer and Black hair cuts
passed bagels and bulletproof liquor
My eyes wide open; they suck in everyone
who wants to get in
permanently

white mama blues

if you ever
tell me
I have a nice ass
again
mama
I'm going to kill you

I remember
my mother
Christmas day 96
ripping the dreadlocks
outta my head
pushing my head down
the sink's wet white hole

I can't breathe   can't breathe
I choke on terror
on her sickness as she hacks through my naps
throws my hair in her toilet
because THEY'RE DIRTY
THAT'S WHY YOU HAVE HEADLICE
THOSE "DREADS" OR WHATEVER YOU CALL THEM
THAT'S WHY THOSE
PEOPLE ALL HAVE LICE
I RAISED YOU BETTER THAN THAT

remembering
10 years of kinky head
brushed straight
2 hours every day under the blowdryer
squirming and twisting as she
makes sure to get every part straight
frizzy anyway
I don't know why she's doing this
feels wrong
but that's just another sign
that I'm fucked up

26

The British empire is alive and well on my head
in 1982,1983, '84, 85, 86
thousands of days of my life

I never even knew I had kinky hair til I was 12
which is how old I was when
she let me wash my own hair
for the first time
I let it dry in the sun
and realized it was curly
so curly
curlier than I ever saw hair being
in Seventeen or on MTV
except on Slash and some of Prince's girls
Maybe I was Latina
or Middle Eastern
It would explain a lot

Frown
I DON'T LIKE YOU HAIR THAT WAY
she is three days crying in her bedroom with the lights off
New England killing frost emotions
til I apologize
With my body she can do
whatever she wants

"I don't have to hit you
I just stop loving you for a few days
and you fall in line."

But it never happened
None of it
ever happened

Don't fuck anybody you wouldn't want to be

I gave up two things this New Year's
I gave up cigarettes and white boys
'cause I figure they're the same thing
taking years off my life   teeth out of my mouth
while they spit down my throat they're the only thing that's going
                                        to save me.
I say basta to years of white boys trying to rub their skin off on me
wanting to see if it slants sideways
or if what they say 'bout colored pussy's really true
especially the kind from that exotic erotic mango sucking east
the kind that's just dark enuf to be sexy
not dark enuf to be scary
Too many years of being the jewel in his crown
Too many years of becoming Italian   Jewish   Portuguese?
cause what else could I be
I'm with him, aren't I?
Because whiteness wants to take
whatever it can

I've had enough of relationships like bad coalition movements
There will be no more International Socialists in this bed
I want somebody whose armpits smell like my grandmother's
kitchen
who aisn't afraid of chili lips burning hers
The tamarind smells from her pussy match mine
and our hair naps into one forest of kinks
Our colors don't clash
as she lies on my earth
sucks coconut cream from my breast
nudges plantain all up in me
something like Kali and Durga must've rocked

But there ain't no twelve step program
for not fucking your way up by your bootstraps anymore
hardly anything telling you you're on the right path
leading broken down into the jungle

not clean and paved into soul death
as you writhe on your bed
trying to shut up that genocide voice
telling you forget   forget   forget who you are
is the most ugly yellow brown wrong thing in the world
if you strangle yourself everything'll be alright
be cause the only visa immigration gives
is for slitting your own throat

but I'm still going back home
This isn't home   we can't go home
but why don't you try making a home in these arms
where you can touch that place their cock never broke
I want you to reach up through my cervix   past my womb
wrap your hands round my heart
no longer
in exile

colorslut

faded in February basement gray, I blow $14.96 on Khlorine from
the MAC counter, searching the racks of puce, ultraviolet and taupe
til I find the one
 that's it, that's perfect   shiny blue sea green ultraviolet
that glows in the dark, gives off sparks   I could say it's like
Negombo Beach at sunset but I never been   but I dream it's true
I accentuate this with a hot pink and burnt orange scarf and the
eyeglasses with violet lenses   this is how I cope with not being
bronzed to light   brown, with not even being dark olive in winter

so girl, when we gonna set up that half desh half honky girls tanning salon
visit? anytime, but only if you promise not to tell anybody   he
laughs, says *can I come too?* at the nude beach the day the UV is up
to 12, we both forgo sunblock   Want to believe the melanin we got
is enough to protect us, longing for shade to come out and play
instead of lumping up in little dark brown dots on fried skin

with each day in the season of color as I get browner, as my hair
kinks out perfect with no need of expensive styling products
or picks or attachments on the blowdryer, I turn into
a different person. Rock my big ass hoops,
settle in

I am not Ellen Degeneres

Some days I feel like a ghost girl
like I died when I was 19
still holding these memories
too real to be true   like a TV movie
My girl friend's boyfriend who shot himself in the head
test results in front of him on the kitchen table
people who've been nodding for a decade now
Girls who blew away in the wind
like the trash they were said to be

What happened to her
who ran away from Salt Lake City Mormon family
to the Sunset Strip to suck dick
and then win a full scholarship
still didn't know how to take care of herself.
We were on Avenue B
drinking King Cobra, wanted weed
and some goth with Dracula teeth bonded on said
don't let her ask for the weed. You,
(she pointed to me) *you'll be okay*
I knew how to look mean and crazy enough

Staring into the face of television
that says queer ten years later
and means perky, blond, perfect
sometimes I feel like a ghost
still walking those streets
renovated beyond recognition
who remembers all the crazy girls
scraping up 99 cents for a forty
a ghost who remembers
that kids like me
still blow away in the wind
unless we grab on tight

You play *love keep us together*
when we're far a-part

as you stare me down at conscious gigs some sistas let you dj
But you didn't love me enough
to make sure your rage
went into a cop or your papi
did you?

Instead
you took that fine-toothed comb of our politics
to rake bloody lines into me
Scream at me for hours
I'm just the same
as some ungrateful white bitch
because I wanted a room of my own
with a door I could lock
against you
Months spent banging your fist
your head   coffee cups you
threw to splinters just above the bed
smashing the mirror in our eyes
that reflected only our sacredness

So now instead of writing beautiful poems
I gotta write down every time you ripped my body in half
so Immigration will be compassionate and humanitarian
Spend my genius finding the perfect words to speak
the way your hands felt wrapped around my throat
the texture of *no you're not fucking going anywhere*
the memory of being that pathetic
of being that woman crawling on a floor
begging to live

You ain't strong brown earth if you bleed
He's an endangered brotha
His fist's not his fault
She said to me, *They're so hurt*
from the coup   the camps   the street & the joint
I say <u>*So are we*</u>
Quoting Assata excuses
nothing

happy IWD!

there's nothing more boring than two femmes hating over a boy
any gender   any color
especially when you said I could fuck him
yet you persist
guess all you could dream was a sidekick
not my naked cunt   bleeding   in yr hand,
much like yours
there's nothing more tired
than 2 femmes
air kissing and clawing each other's hearts to shreds
we knew best how to do it cuz after all
                              once we loved each other
Bad night? the waitress says
better than some
worse than most
waiting for the paycheck to clear
so I can buy myself flowers
I couldn't love you hard enough
to stop you from cutting your hand off
the first time I made it itch

so what the fuck does conscious mean anyway

It's that gnawed bone moment
when you realize "The Community" will do nothing
to stop him from showing up at your backdoor
 in the middle of the night
with the rifle he bought for the revolution
safety off
It's personal not political   they don't know what
to do 'bout you
lying bitch

Then you think:
if they are the only thing that can save my life
and they won't
are they betrayers   are the family
what good are they?
Do we need any more Eldridge Cleavers?
as we try to *do it right* this time
something we want
with every cell
Our last chance not to fuck up.

but sometimes
we want to close our eyes
jack off to pictures of radical disneyland
not watch as we gnaw our own
flesh into meat

this ain't the time

Hoarding hours
to stare out the window
feel like shit
& play that same damn Lauryn Hill over & over again
I want to give you back everything
you ever gave me
cowrie shell bracelet   Franz Fanon w/inscriptions
the pictures of your boots
kicking me curled up fetal
 in your closet
This ain't the time to remember
all the love we used to cook up on a one burner stove
how I used to come up behind you up yr nipples & twist
press against yr ass as you gasped and fried me *platano*
grease popping little stars in your arm
this isn't the time to remember what was
good what was all I remembered
for too long

evil bitch 3, the final chapter

Keep expecting the soundtrack to come up on Toni
 saying *he wasn't man enuf for me*
as your new woman and her friend look at me
like *hey there's that crazy dyke bitch*
made his life so hard
and don't brothers already have enough to deal with
I wanna scream *why'd you marry him*
 I know where he's been
but I don't   wish this on anybody
knowing every time you look at me
you're still looking
for the one thing I'll do wrong
that justifies whatever comes next

Someone needs to write a For Dummies book about how to handle
these unique conscious community social situations,
like when you, your girlfriend, the abusive ex, his new wife
and her two best friends are all in the front row of
a Saul Williams concert
which is 75% white people
and all six of us wanna pump our fists
crack the frozen wastelands of the north
but you're still looking at me out the corner of your eye
like
you ruined everything
just by being alive

Two years later
I did not die
you come as a stranger to me
because you are
I don't say anything to you because if I did – anything –
 it wouldn't be too long
before I would be back curled up fetal
 around the sounds of you screaming
throwing myself numb between your fist and the wall

Only goddess ever spoke to you was between my thighs
You told me so that you'd tried so many times
to light candles, touch her earth
and she never would come down roll over into you
wrap her arms round yr waist
and whisper the secret you most needed to know

It is true that men who
can quote Angela on demand   & are willing to eat pussy
are enough of a rarity in this town
they can look like angels descending when they come
but if the man I fell in love with
saw you coming down the street,
that soft eyed angel with the big-ass fro,
I don't know
if he'd puke, kill you or kill himself
knowing that's what he'd become
I got so much guts
You got none

inflammatory

if one more woman says
"I wrote this for my best friend
but I'd never read it to her cause she'd say,
damn, girl, r u a lezzzzbian or something?"
I'm gonna do more than grab
my girl's hand
if one more girl   missionary possession
always talking about Mumia but never her sisters oppression
announces an all women's conference at the break but then blushes
& says *ummmmmmmmmmmm*
don't worry... this doesn't mean we don't like men!
I'm gonna cry   die   throw dishes
weep in anybody's arms
If one more queer press gets bought out by Harry Potter
if one more girl I used to know disappears
                                        like she's never been
I'm gonna cry   die   smash all my dishes
I mean there's some dumb part of me that can't stop standing
saying   *but don't they care about the revolution?*
incredulous
when spoken word meets conscious easy listening
the words could mean anything
but let me be clear:
I'm clear I'm the revolution
just as much
as you

when kali and oya met

Sisters still love each other very much
even when they don't talk for months

It's a lot harder to be a sister than just a girl friend
You go from coffee to gossip fitting safe in each other's pockets
to silent simultaneous radar finding each other at four AM.
Giggle over $5 curry chicken from the Mr. Jerk
that was there before the mall came
Conspiring in fall parks at 3 in the morning
in between five hour coffees   caucus meetings   trips to the joint
Eyes locked   hair locking
stolen groceries   Cigarettes over ital
Held hands over done wrong girlfriends
while eating *vatalapam* and chai
We joked   said cheers
to the cane fields and tea plantations
When I stayed in the hood you moved from
I couldn't watch the sari cloth in your window flap
on my bike ride home   anymore

Desi diva
you were my home
between flights
Cousins once removed
Runaways   we found each other
in my roach kitchen   cooking Christmas dinner.
You said I looked just like your favorite cousin
My heart's cunt clenched shut around you
We thought this would be simple   Love
Watching   as you found that girl
who kissed you neck   called you angel
left a bruise on your thigh
and a thousand roses at your door.
but our glances   one click of the tongue
tore each other to shreds

We were
dangling from the same cord
pulse beating in our throats
Then
we both saw the light
change

& stepped out
without each other
but still beloved
because, you know

sisters still love each other very much
even when they aren't sisters
any more

crazy girl on red bike

why do girls always go I'd asked you
a few days before
you said *because girls are always moving*

double take every bike making sure it's not you
there's good crazy
and bad crazy
and right now that's you
I'll be brave tomorrow
but right now
I'll avoid that coffee shop

good sistas

Good sistas don't have I Heart My Cunt stickers on their bikes
wear their bras as club wear or their leather on the Mumia march.
Good sistas don't shave the dreads
they don't wrap
                    eat roast pork when the moon makes them crazy
don't chain smoke when their best friend's in town
cuz that's the only way   they know how to talk
Don't look like or be a ho   don't
lick pussy or dick & talk bout it
don't bare their ass over a park bench
when the sun is still warm   or the moon is full
Good sistas are celibate as nuns
pledging their life to Talib & hemp bars 'steada Jesus.

The girls I know are none of the above
We mama revolutions at the table and streetcorner
with our *I heart my cunt* stickers
our bras and our leather
eating lots of roast pork
when the moon makes us crazy
Remember to feed us first
and rock us to sleep wrapped up tight
as we mama revolutions
with our chipped turquoise nails
fiiiiiiiine

mi papi maricon

Baby, can you lend me your copy of *City of Night*
now that you've traded it for *The Final Call?*
Now that you who cruised the piers' black-eyed brown boys
when we were lovers   now that you
decided everything queer came from that different shore.
You went from fishnet shirt fem
to Panther leather, fake patwa and pink glasses
tryin to make your blue eyes brown
but I always saw their color
The fights we fought over who passed more,
the man who smiled at us talkin spanish in the project elevator
who said *I bet she taught you that.*
The way you screamed me away from you
for being four shades browner
I saw kinky blond brown & indio eyes
 swore everyone else could too

I like 'em brown yella puerto rican & haitian
we all yelled   threw our hands up
                                        my friend's 23rd birthday jam
You were 600 miles away on the phone screaming
how could I want the girl in him
gotta start pumping again
                don't wanna look like a punk if I go back inside
Sticks up the ass at 12 and cocks the same
Did white men holding twenty dollars folding money
did white men grabbing hot Latino ass ruin you for me

Baby why don't you give me back yr copy of *City of Night*
now that you've traded it in for *The Final Call*
to be a righteous endangered brown man
not a faggot
Only okay to be that if you're white
or dead like Marlon and Essex
Does your father finally approve
forget your blond fro, eyelashes, gentle face at six
I'm keeping on running
without you

44

abortion poem

All this woman juice gone sour
all this semen 'n egg   blastocysts
Red wine linings turned to hangovers
shining shivering   thinking
I guess I got what I deserved

At 8:30 in the AM
I jump off my bike
and perform my first job duty of the day
As it says in the employee handbook,
"As you approach the clinic
scan the rooftops for snipers
If you see none unlock the front door and proceed"

Sometimes I wear my I Do Bad Things t-shirt
We play Lauryn,
fast forward past "To Zion"

Here I am in this room
With her
17 years old, size 2
17 weeks
she thinks six
wearing booty jeans and a
What Would Jesus Do wristband.
She shouldn't have this
child of uncle or rape   I can tell
the way she won't say anything
or sex cause it was the thing to do
with all the lights off
The way she asks me now *please*
Can you turn the lights down?
She shouldn't
have this child
She shouldn't have another ghost circling
her head either

45

I want to tell the spirit hovering
next time, when it's right
bury her under a cedar tree
not leave her unfinished

I talk to brown woman after woman
who would have this baby
if she'd had something else
besides a night job and a day job
and sleep from four to six in the afternoon
Bottom down, snaps the doc
 I know if she keeps moving
it can pierce the uterus
I squeeze her hand, stroke her hair   Breathe,
girl, breathe
Leaving the recovery room
still groggy from Vicodin, she holds me tight

I remember them all
the woman crying after,
so glad she didn't almost die like her sister
the Pentacostal woman
who said   *well, I know I'm going to hell for this*
But what can you do

I dream a day when every one of us
knows the shape of our clit
the exact taste of our cunts
the moment we are fertile
and exactly what it takes
to make us come
a day when there is time enough
for us to bless and bury
what we leave behind
where there is choice
enough for every brown women
wringing life into this world

1997-1999

the guy who let me be seventeen cents short
on my bulk food store food
making pancakes outta 46 cents a pound mix
for breakfast, lunch and dinner
all the people who jammed open back doors of the bus
one chicken leg a week
the lady at the low-income program at the Y
wants to know my budget $600 a month. $525 rent.
what is the extra ten dollars?   I have a coffee, buy soap.
you can pay a dollar more this year,
she says, *you can afford it*
It's a good thing Toronto is a city you can walk
because you will walk everywhere
Trying to run a prison justice   magazine
when nobody in the joint can pay subscriptions and you are
walking across town to the apartment with
the computer and stamps
hoping the angry old anarchist waiting for retirement
will defrost some leftovers for your dinner
your lover is poor for the revolution but his parents send
$800 a month
now that he's no longer on the street
he gives you some of his oranges
from Kensington Market, sends you the free food box
that feeds you months of vegetables
The free phone at the cafe
lasts just long enough for you to get a visa, then two bad jobs,
then another
miss Pride so you can read Tarot at the arts fair and make $200
telling peoples' futures
You get one
just in time
just before they cut it off and install an emergency-use-only
pay phone.

citizenship is something you hold

somewhere there's a recycling box
full up to the brim with blue
7 day protection candles
I burned

menstrual blood smeared
above the door jamb
a rusty iron pipe under
my pillow

a stadium full of all the open mics I couldn't attend
because you did

old scars
healed with
homegrown calendula
ropy like a vein
well used
thick like a road
I walked down
to this place

confrontation day

the day before I confronted my family, when the twenty-two page letter was all printed out from the Stylewriter II but not yet slipped in the manila envelope, I lay in bed and dreamed. I dreamed, lying on two flat junkpicked futons, with the railroad tracks clicking away like ocean behind me, that I was all alone in the middle of the night sky. I was floating there surrounded by blackness, ink dark. I could feel that all my ancestors, my dead grandparents, my uncle who died in a car crash after making it home from Korea, my other uncle who'd died of cirrhosis of the liver, they all surrounded me. and ones much older.

I thought "Is what I'm doing right? Is all I think is true actually right?"

I didn't expect to get an answer   But from all of them in that circle, I got this booming "YES"

And I was falling, so many million miles a second, back down, down,rushing towards the oceans and continents til I hit

I woke up with a thump as I was thrown back on the bed

**I didn't want the end times
to be like this:
9/11 in seven slams**

1. HOW DID *YOUR* LIFE CHANGE AFTER SEPTEMBER 11????

After everything I've made it through, it made me want to die
I didn't want to live in fascism live on TV
staring me dead in the eye with a retina scanner
and my prints on universal ID
I didn't want to live after they preemptively nuked
a place   not where I'm from
but mine nonetheless
We are all Afghani now   all us brown folks
Nepali to native
it doesn't matter to them

   2.

I saw *Bush says: Expect attacks in the few day*
Then the bus was out of service
Then the next bus came by
The driver looked at me
 the only one at the stop   and kept going
I was fifteen minutes late for pay what you can yoga
They didn't let me in
Said it would disrupt the spiritual balance of the class
I walked in the rain to stare at another screen
and ended up on a payphone
making my lover break a date with his other
I needed him to calmly listen to me telling him
where the will was
and who I didn't want invited to the funeral
Sometimes living because of fresh mango juice
and Assata's voice saying
"the only way to live on this planet
with any human   dignity at the moment
is to struggle"

seems like confetti
over land mined stumps
of flesh

3. I'M NOT MUSLIM BUT I COULD PLAY ONE ON TV!

see I'm used to not looking Sri Lankan
to never being profiled as what I actually am
I'm used to light skinned   green eyed
This has been the mode minority minute
 and it's over now!
I'm used to working it   to get my friends cab rides
and free passes across the border

Four days after the world blew up I was on my way home
and I decided to stop at the Price Chopper. I needed to load up on
as many ten pound bags of rice and dhal as possible in case
the world blew up again.
So there's me with my halal chicken and Mr. Gouda's dhal 'n
black-eyed peas that's got Arab, Hebrew Spanish *and* English labels
and there's checkout gal pulling each one past the scanner
real slow
and she looks at it
and looks at me
and then pulls another one past
and looks at it
and looks at me
real slow
And I wanted to scream
YEAH   THAT'S RIGHT BITCH   I CAN MAKE A BOMB
ME, THIS HALAL CHICKEN AND A NOSERING
MAKE A BOMB!

4. HOW TO TELL GOOD TURBANS FROM BAD TURBANS

cuz y'know you can't tell them apart
the Muslims and the Indians
hell, the Indians and the Indians
the japs and the chinks

those people all so tricky!
and we let them be
but now is the time for clarity!
let's wipe 'em out
like every store of anthrax we ever
made to use against them
but until then   remember
GOOD SIKHS HAVE ROUNDED, NEATLY WRAPPED TURBANS
"THE EVIL ONES" HAVE POINTED, SLOPPILY WRAPPED ONES

5. today is the day when:

the bus didn't stop for me today
my best friend's mother got a traffic cone thrown at her head today
my little brother got jacked on the way from the subway today
my ex got held up at gunpoint for four hours today
my fingerprints are gonna be on a card today
we're all gonna be terrorists today
we all need to get facelifts today
I'm so fucking scared to say anything today

Before
I was thinking too much of myself
or just enough
the way I might not be allowed to think of myself
ever again

6. They don't put us in internment camps anymore,
we just don't leave the house

We don't leave our houses
cuz when we do things happen
like me in the $3/hour internet cafe
surrounded by twelve year old white boys playing Counterstrike
screaming "just carpet bomb him, dude, it don't matter!"

We don't leave the house
so we don't end up like

that Cherokee woman   health care worker
bludgeoned to death by three drunk white boys on her reservation
as they screamed "GO BACK TO WHERE YOU COME FROM"
Do you know her name?
We know
we won't
end up on
the news

7.

Maybe it's time to drop the self tanner
and go for the bleach!
Now that, for once, olive might be scarier than black
now that even the most inauthentic halfbreed is the most suspect

Maybe the apocalypse is gonna make me buy shoes
lots and lots of shoes
and six dollar juice bar drinks
I've never been able to afford
but what
the
hell

or maybe
this one's gonna make me
FIGHT HARDER THAT I'VE EVER FOUGHT BEFORE

9/11/02

7:30 AM train to New York
 and everyone has an American flag
except this boy at the ticket booth
who has glitter steel nails   hanging dreads
a look in his eye

He says to me
Four of my queer desi friends
have killed themselves
since September 11
Four
It's like, if you're queer and brown
go snort coke up a rolled up flag,
if you brown and political
 don't talk 'bout your cock
and where you stick it   we serious now.

I want to do what my grandmother did
in another time of terror
after spending my whole life mocking her:
pass as the darkest shade of white available
bury gold under the mattress   get approved by Mastercard
cultivate multiple passports
& get the last boat out
to squat carefully in a land
that is not mine

I want to keep the Dutch name on my passport
I want to be a cute Italian girl
the INS agent thinks could be his daughter
I want to lie careful   be quiet
crawl into a hole of TV
and girlfriend and food
cooked for all of us
who are too scared
to go to the demonstration

But it's too late:
he doesn't think I look like his daughter
I don't look Dutch enough for the passport to be mine
I don't know which finger the ring should go on
I am crossing the border with my girlfriend not my husband
In my head the ice room waiting for me
not veiled   not turbaned
not Muslim or Arab
but the beige center line
where everything could be fine   or fall apart
I do not control my abusers
One bad day
and anything could happen
I smile tight
and hand over my passport

biogenocide

"This is an active war on our children. Our genes are our sacred right to pass down to our children. No one can take that away."
— DEBORAH HARRY, Indigenous Coalition
Against Biocolonialism

1.
One half
one quarter
one eighth
one sixteenth
straight hair   thin noses   blue eyes:
after four generations humid kinks   lie flat
after eight generations my ex is not breed like me
but another white girl with a Native great-great-grandmother
possibly

2.
We say we're still brown so fierce, us breed girls   say we are
still our brown raped grandmothers, not our white adoptive ones
      say it over and over again that we ain't hybrid corn that
kills butterflies, spliced far far away from dirt   the world
is our laboratory, matching white father X with brown mother Y in
people's iris scanning our faces, dissecting combinations of eyelash,
nose, cheekbones, lips

3.
The Irish red hair, Tamil kinks and frizz, Sinhalese almond eyes and
bad singing, Ukranian potato face: I've passed through them all
had red hair and blue eyes when I was four   I wait with hand
on belly already hard dreaming child yet to come, what genes get
lulled to sleep, curled up in a ball will stretch and rise?

The universe splits, Shakti spins the earth on one finger, lightning
fuses sperm and egg together, random eye glint & cocked brow 'n
hip   the stories begin again.

4.
I lie with my white boyfriend whose cock can do everything but
spit seed into me, 'cept there's times when I'm convinced I'll have

56

the second virgin birth, bring the next messiah forth outta nothing
more than silicone and wish   "you're lucky she's not a bio boy"
said my friend   yeah, cause if she was there's nothing says I
wouldn't have that child, that child outta love who could dissapear
outta love to nothing.

Once I thought I would find a fine brown man with good politics
and give my child
that gift
give her back what was stolen from me

Colonialism created the first
genetically modified organisms
white sperm injected into dark egg
They think we'll
smile faster   bend over quicker
follow in line like it's bred into us
Instead
our mutant *quilombos* take over the earth
we run through the streets
screaming our true names
the ones they'll never
ever
learn to pronounce
We be as untamable as our hair
as the jungle they try to synthesize
We be red rebel gurls
Michelle Cliff, Chrystos
and me
We make new families
not tragedies

This bed is no laboratory
this house isn't Honduras
this bed is choice
cocked brow and hip
spit and sperm mixed with a finger
whatever's next.

how not to be bitter
(mama's recipe)

don't screech I AM NOT
BITTER to your 13 year old
daughter while slamming
on the brakes
in traffic when
she asks you why
you are

don't stay in a town
where you can't drink the water
 & the air makes
people's hair fall out
on a regular basis

where there is no music
you like to dance to
either recorded live
or the beating of your heart

don't get more into
Lifetime for Women reruns
than your own life

don't thirst for moisture
for so long you dry out
a little water   aloe
cocoa butter
is all you need

pretty light skin dream

1.
Neither of us looks like Mya
or Aishwarya Rai
We are big butt girls   didn't get the little noses
just the straight hair   strong hips
big feet
We cannot rock our lightness into the gold
our men search for
not   Bollywood princess
nor   fade cream ad
but
"Spanish night is on Saturday"
from the Revolution Books guy
as we both smile
turn
& switch our big butts
out the door

2.
We like our women light – but not as light as you!
My story
is one white mother   one brown father
mother is white and working class, usually Irish
father is a first son gone bad
 who got a wandering eye in London
they live in the mother's city, not the father's
His family is phone calls, blue aerogram letters
daughter is almost many things: almost a woman of color,
almost white, almost dark
visibility depends on many factors:
variable humidity, smog alerts, UV,
seasonal changes and pollen count
and most importantly
how those looking
know how to see

3.
Sometimes the mix doesn't take
and we can't dance   sing   make aloo gobi.
We flunk all the tests
hybrid seeds are subjected to
so are we useless?
If we aren't
some magic unique flower
making a biotech firm millions.

If we are useful
only to ourselves
we see each other
our visibility a constant
unaffected
by smog or
UV

I am a contradiction to your definition

It was already a shitty-ass day and I was riding
 my adult tricycle home in the rain
the one that read, in that bad time
cranky brown queer girl against war
you ran out to tell me like somebody should
"you're not really brown   you know"
because you know
you know me better than I do
you always
know us better
than we do

And I coulda said a lot of things
like"yes I am" or"browner than you" or
"I'm the same color as Iraqi women"

but you're the great-great-grandson
of the man who invented the auction block
I wonder if you know the words your grandpa invented
like *coyote*   *mestiza*
mullata   eurasian   half-breed
I do

Five centuries later blood quantum is an concept you made up
to push people off our nations   reservations
and I know that brown is a city
a continent   a world
that stretches far past what you can see
from olive sunset to mahogany sunrise
from the girl who wants to be darker
to the girl with the bluest eyes

Brown is the soil
of an unlived land
whose dirt I scatter
wherever I go
How we darkeye each other across the room
is something you'll never know
You'll never know us

You don't know how to plant this soil
give it up   this food is too hot for you
and you won't cut down this
or any
of these olive trees
still bearing fruit

for Ami and Amar Puri

restorative justice

On the way back from New Orleans with my female boyfriend
we've almost made it through
until he tells me
You have to go over there
nods me over to that plexiglass soundproof chamber
where all the ones who aren't
real Americans get to go

and I think to myself
What if every time they pulled over one of us
we got to grab one of them?
What if every time any agent of immigration
who ever probed us with questions
like fingers put where they don't belong,
what if every time they called one of us
down a long beige hallway
leading to another long beige hallway
taking you to a place   none of us want to go

What if every time we crossed a border we never made up
and they started up with
Why do you have a Quar'an in your bag?
Have you ever been on welfare?
Where is your husband? Why aren't you traveling with him?
We could start asking them questions
important ones, like
How do you touch your child
with the same hands that ripped open
my bags, my Qua'ran, my stories?

What if we could bring them to that long beige place
and make them unlock all the ones who didn't make it through?
keep going   open the doors at Guantanimo and the Celebrity Inn
what if we could jump behind that counter
get on the PA and announce

It is hereby declared
that all borders are bullshit
and starting today
we   will never stand on this line
sweating terror
ever
again

inspired by June Jordan's poem, "Poem About Police Brutality"

I have three photographs

When the Japanese bombed Malaysia
my grandparents got out on the last boat
They were a middle class teacher/ engineer family
but all they took with them was ere my uncle Jeremy
my unborn father
and two books of photographs

Jeremy was four
He was blond and blue-eyed
and my grandparents felt like they'd hit the genetic jackpot
He died of bomb shock when they reached Colombo
My father has black hair and brown skin
He has my eyes

The first photograph is in sepia
A middle class Burgher family
in 1931 Colombo
My great-grandfather is round and brown in a waistcoat
my great-grandmother has a mouth so tight you could fit it in
                                                    a bottle cap
but oh, their daughters!
My grandmother
at twenty-two
Black Jackie Alvis Samarasinha
of the Women's Franchise Union
her sisters my great aunties Reenee and Christabel
In 1931
they have bobbed hair
and are showing their ankles
They have bicycles
and picket signs
They are the Wild Alvis Girls
In that time of strikes   secret lovers
Burgher, Tamil, Sinhalese, Muslim women
all standing up against colonialism
They look right at the camera

like nothing
will ever
stop them
One sister even smiles
My grandmother
looks absolutely
furious
with everything

My second photograph is a polaroid.
It is 1969
and my father is vogueing by a VW bus
in London
He is beautiful
He looks like the biggest faggot in the world
and he is,
My dad is hanging in London
where all the ex-colonials are in 1969
saying "we are here because you were there"
and my mother is a milltown girl in a miniskirt
who has just won a Fullbright
after 8 years of getting her master's in night school
They are going to walk down the aisle
to Peter Paul and Mary
and when my grandparents
come to meet them
the first thing *appamma* will say
at the end of the Heathrow runway
is
"We had another son you know.
He had blond hair and blue eyes."

In 2000 I am twenty-five
I am in San Francisco
at the queer desi conference
and there are seven of us
seven queer Sri Lankan women!
 I see a tall butch woman in a green shirt
who has my eyes

I say
"Are you Burgher?"
and she says "Yes"
for the first time in my life
Later we stand for the camera
cinnamon, milk tea and ebony
and we know we can do anything

I dream mixed blood bodies that
gave birth to revolutions
that faded to sad stillness
I am all the stories my family
never knew how to speak

sweet water, 3/19/03*

Love is strong as death itself... its flashes are flashes
of fire, a flame of the Eternal.
Floods cannot quench love, rivers cannot drown it.
                                    – The Song of Songs

I am pouring sweet water on my altar for you
praying that this prayer matters
Take my seven day candle out to recycling
cause none of it
did
shit
I delete all entries in my mailbox
containing the words   *humanitarian crisis   civilian*
deaths   heat weapon   infrastructure overwhelmed
Staring into the computer at work,
I see scorched air rising from Baghdad
bombs with wings like small butterflies
seeking a seven-year-old's head   a mother's swollen belly
my cervix pinches with cramps
I feel this shit   blowing up my womb
like the fresh c-section scars of the women
who rushed to give birth
before the bombing started

But no, I'm not marching to the consulate today
I stay home   light another candle
I don't have any gun to fight them with
except my tongue   my heart
I am pouring sweet water on my altar for you
knowing that this prayer is all I can do
and remembering
survivors survive
whether they want us to
or not

*for the people of Iraq

68

Notes

Fifty Years

"Emptying the fishtank" – technique of quieting unrest by murdering every person in a given area

papi maricon

City of Night – by John Rechy, classic work about queer men and public sex.
The Final Call – newspaper of the Nation of Islam

I didn't want the end times to be like this: 9/11 in seven slams

Kimberley Lowe, 21, an enrolled member of the Creek nation, was chased by three drunk white men who yelled "Go back to where you came from!" before beating her to death on September 17, 2001. She was one of many victims of the frenzy of hate crimes against people perceived to be Arab or Muslim.

Acknowledgments

Grateful acknowledgment is made to these publications, where some of the poems (or earlier versions of them) first appeared: *Big Boots:* "Crazy girl on red bike"; *Critical Times:* "I am a contradiction to your definition"; *Lodestar Quarterly:* "Sweet water"; *Mizna:* "9/11 in seven slams"; *Thirdspace:* "pretty light skinned dream"; *Trikone:* "Restorative justice"

I would also like to thank the Toronto Arts Council, The Canada Council for the Arts, Norcroft and Artstarts for the gifts of money and time that made this book possible.

Thanks and shoutouts:

Without Bushra Rehman's generous brilliance as an editor this book would have sucked a lot harder. No cute little gimics that worked at open mics in 1998! Thanks ma, for this and everything else. I can't wait to do the same with your next book.

Suheir Hammad's skills as a teacher at Voices of Our Nations 2005, her compassion, fierce belief in her students and X-ray vision, created the place where many of these poems were written and many more were transformed. Thank you so much for teaching me to write love poems, for telling me to love the dorky four year old inside. For telling me to go to the water and for not being able to wait.

Thank you to Nurjehan Aziz at TSAR for publishing radical South Asian books and poetry when few will. Thank you to Chamindika Wanduragala for being a deliciously visionary artist and for creating the cover piece. Thank you Anna Cammileri, Nalo Hopkinson and Elizabeth Ruth for mentoring me as a writer even when you didn't know you were. Thanks to all the bookstore babes at Toronto Women's Bookstore and everyone at Desh Pardesh, Artwallah, Diasporadics, Desi-Q, Lotus Roots, Mayworks, the INCITE/ Color of Violence community, Bar 13, Bluestockings, Rivers of Honey, Gendercrash, Asian American Writer's Workshop, Masala Masti

Mendhi, Asian Arts Initiative, the API Spoken Word Summit family, Nomy Lamm, Diaspora/Flow, Bao Phi and The Loft, Bookstore of the Americas, Lodestar Quarterly, SAMAR, Trikone, Mizna, Colorlines and Bitch for supporting my work with places to perform and publish. Many thanks to Jamie Munkatchy for working with me to create the first, handmade version of CG, emailing proofs from Brooklyn to Toronto and sewing books together on the couch.

Thanks to the writers and artists who feed and teach me: Hana Abdul, Bushra Rehman, Trish Salah, Karene Silverwoman, Andre Lancaster, Marian Yalini Thambynayagam, Dulani, Pireeni Sunderlingam, Varuni Tiruchelvam, Ching-In Chen, Trey Anthony, Macho Cabrera Estevez, Lamya El-Chidiac, Celeste K. Chan, Karleen Pendleton-Jimenez, Gein Wong, Ruthann Lee, Jin Huh, Nasreen Khan, Anurima Bannerji, Victor Tobar, Mirha Soleil-Ross, Rosina Kazi, Reena Katz, Zavisha Chromicz, Zoe Whitall, Nomy Lamm, Mango Tribe. To the youth of Pink Ink for being a constant inspiration.

To the Sri Lankans who make a new way: Marian Yalini, Pireeni, Varuni Tiruchelvam, Mayuran Tiruchelvam, Chamindika Wanduragala and Pradeepa Jeeva, Gitanjali and Suvendrini Lena, Annanda DeSilva, Sharmini Fernando, Sharmini Peries, Rosanna Flamer-Caldera and Tammi Flamer, Kumaran Nesiah, Karla Zombro, Harini Sivalingam and Kshama Ranawana.

To Hana Abdul and Eowyn Jordison for being family and heart. To the family I have made, in Toronto and around the world.